USING FILM
IN THE SOCIAL STUDIES

William B. Russell III

University Press of America,® Inc.
Lanham · Boulder · New York · Toronto · Plymouth, UK

CONTENTS

Contents

LIST OF TABLES

PREFACE & OVERVIEW

This book was written to help promote appropriate film use in the social studies. Using film as an enhancement tool is very effective and has been found to have many positive outcomes on student learning and interest. However, for film to be effective it must be used appropriately. This book provides a rationale for using film in the social studies, as well as a research based model, the *Russell Model for Using Film*, for using film appropriately in the classroom.

Although most teachers use film in the classroom, many have never received formal instruction on how to effectively and appropriately use film in the classroom. Moreover, many teachers use film as a time-filler with no educational value and break many laws, regarding copyright, when doing so. This book provides readers with a model for using film and covers the legal issues surrounding film use in the classroom.

Chapter one, "Introduction" will provide readers with a foundation and a rationale for using film. As well, the *Russell Model for Using Film* is discussed in detail. The four stage model will help ensure appropriate film use.

Chapter two, "Legal Issues" will provide readers with the legal issues surrounding film use in the classroom. Specifically, the United States Code on Copyright, the Fair Use policy, and the Recording of Off-Air Broadcasting.

Chapter three, "Review of Literature" will provide readers a brief historical look at research on film in education and the outcomes film has on student learning and interest.

Chapter four, "Research Study" details a research study of how Florida social studies teachers use film in the classroom. The study tests three separate hypotheses.

Chapter five, "Results of Study" discusses the results of research study, described in chapter four. Each hypothesis is presented separately.

Chapter six, "Discussion of Results" discusses the results of the study and how it impacts social studies teachers and how film is used in the classroom. The results of each hypothesis are discussed separately.

Chapter seven, "Conclusion" provides readers with a summary of the major points discussed throughout this book.

Remember, when used correctly, film is a powerful and visually stimulating tool. However, film must be used to enhance the lesson, not as the lesson.

William B Russell III, Ph.D.
University of Mississippi, December 2006

ACKNOWLEGMENTS

I would like to express a sincere thank you to the many people and institutions that made this book possible.

A special thank you goes to Florida State University and the University of Mississippi. I would also like to thank the Statistical Consulting Center at Florida State University for the statistical assistance.

I am greatly indebted to all of the school districts, schools, and teachers who participated in this study, Thank You.

I would like to express my deepest appreciation to my wife, Catie, my son, William, and my dog, Zeus, for loving and helping me throughout this process. Plus, I would like to thank my mother, Laura Puckett, for being the best mom in the world and for believing in me. I would also like to thank the following: William Puckett, William Russell, The Kwiatkowski Family, The Hudgins Family, Liz's Family, Ashley's Family, The McClellan Family, All the Russell families, The Litton Family, The Kelly Family, The Leonard Family, The Rice Family, The Pellegrino Family, The LeJuene Family, and Kenton Williams.

I would also like to express a sincere thank you to Robert Gutierrez, John Lunstrum, Jim Jones, and Kay Picart for all their support and encouragement while conducting the research.

A special thank you goes to Anthony Pellegrino for all of the support and encouragement and to Jace Hargis for being such a great resource.

ONE

INTRODUCTION

An average student is said to spend "about five and half hours a day using media (5.29) – more than 38 hours a week" (Kaiser Family Foundation, p.9). On the average, over three hours a day is devoted to just television and videos (Kaiser Family Foundation, 1999). These findings demonstrate that children have more exposure to films, television, and other media than school. To help fuse the two opposing forces together, teachers have been using film as an instructional enhancement tool for teaching their respective content throughout the twentieth century. Some content areas lend themselves to using film in the curriculum. From personal experience, the social studies curriculum is the most notorious for using film.

The use of film by social studies teachers varies depending on numerous variables. Uncontrollable variables such as equipment, money, availability of film, and district and state policies all impact an individual social studies teacher's use of film in the classroom. However, when social studies teachers do have the opportunity to use film, controllable variables, can include what to show, when to show it, why to show it, how much to show, and how to assess corresponding student achievement.

Teachers using films in the classroom can be seen as an effective strategy (Paris, 1997) or as a waste of precious instructional time (Reform K-12, 2004). *Reform K-12* is an online chat room by which teachers, parents, administrators, and others discuss varying educational issues. One complaint described an irate parent whose child had viewed over sixty-seven Hollywood movies in a special education classroom from August to November (four months) of a single school year. Another complaint describes how schools have used films as non-instructional time, allowing Fridays to become "Movie Friday" (Reform K-12, 2004). These concerns are genuine and are serious setbacks for teachers who use film in the classroom, because it gives teaching with film a negative image. Furthermore, when film is misused and abused in the classroom, every step that has been taken by researchers and teachers to make film a powerful and useful tool is almost negated, instantly.

For all intent and purposes the term film refers to the following: movies, videos, documentaries, and other audio/visual materials. Furthermore, the format can include film strips, DVD, VHS, laser disc, and streaming video.

Theoretical Framework

When using film in the social studies classroom, instructional goals like reasoning, critical thinking, retention and understanding, self-regulation, and reflection of the curriculum should be used to maximize student learning. These constructivist goals can be achieved by using film appropriately in the social studies classroom. To reach these goals, film has been shown to help develop students' historical understanding (Allen, 2005) by providing visual images of historical events.

Film is an enhancement tool for the curriculum, it is not the curriculum, and so by using film as a tool, teachers allow students to take ownership in learning. By taking an element (film) that has real life application and incorporating it into the curriculum students will have higher levels of interest in the lesson. Lessons that use real life application are often found in the constructivist learning theory.

Using authentic activities in the classroom help to achieve instructional goals like retention and understanding, reasoning, and critical thinking (Driscoll, 2000). Authentic activities can include the following methods of instruction micro-worlds, problem-based learning, hypermedia (media), role-plays, debates, and collaborative learning. Furthermore, Allen (2005) explains that examining films can promote historical thinking and awareness of historical prospective.

Engle (1960; 2003) stressed decision-making as the heart of social studies education. Pressing that students learn the decision making process, instead of content memorization. Film can help provoke meaningful inquiry of a historical event, thus allowing students to make insightful decisions based on what they viewed and what the teacher does to support the curriculum.

According to Allen (2005) using film in the classroom can help students develop historical thinking skills. However if teachers fail to use film appropriately, the ability to help students develop historical thinking skills will be lost. Historical thinking skills are extremely important, so important that in 1994, The National Center for History in Schools (NCHS) developed five standards for historical thinking:

1) Chronological Thinking
2) Historical Comprehension
3) Historical Analysis and Interpretation
4) Historical Research Capabilities
5) Historical Issues-Analysis and Decision-Making

Purpose

The purpose of this book is to provide social studies educators with a research-based example of how social studies teachers are using film in the classroom. The research study presented in chapter three examined social studies teachers' practices for using film in the classroom. Studying how social studies teachers use film in the classroom helped determine, 1) if teachers are using film to enhance instruction and learning in a lesson, 2) if the proper rules and regulations are being followed, and/or 3) if film is being used as a reward or time-filler.

Historians have found that film images impact and influence a person's perspective of history (O'Connor & Jackson, 1988), thus it is important to understand how social studies teachers use film in the classroom. Furthermore, historians have also found that history on film can be an accurate interpretation of history (Rosenstone,

1995) and that film can bring students closer to the people and events that they are studying (Matz & Pingatore, 2005).

The Use of Film

The use of film in the social studies classroom can be an effective strategy for enhancing instruction and teaching the social studies content (Wise, 1939). For film to be effective in the social studies classroom, teachers must properly implement the use of film. Lankford (1992) described a generic model for teachers to follow when using film in the classroom. The generic model included 1) a previewing activity, 2) viewing the film, and 3) post-viewing activity.

The *Russell Model for Using Film*

The *Russell Model for Using Film* is a four-stage model that was developed using the generic model as a base. Using personal teaching experiences, relevant literature, quantitative data collected in the research study described in chapter three, and qualitative data collected in an unpublished research study, the key components necessary for using film effectively in the classroom to maximize student performance and learning were formulated.

Many teachers use film and think they use it effectively, but they do not follow the research-based guidelines for using film as laid out in the *Russell Model for Using Film* (see Table 1.1).

Russell Model for Using Film
1. The Preparation Stage
2. The Pre-Viewing Stage
3. Watching the Film Stage
4. The Culminating Activity Stage

Table 1.1 *Russell Model for Using Film*

Stage 1: The Preparation Stage

The preparation stage is the most important stage of the *Russell Model for Using Film.*
This is the planning stage of the model. The preparation stage includes the following, but is not limited to the following:
(* Denotes required activities)

- Create lesson plans that incorporate film, while still meeting instructional goals/objectives, state standards, national standards, and that adheres to all legal requirements *
- Preview the film! Instructors must preview all films before using a film in the classroom *
- Create a specific pre-viewing activity (see stage 2)*
- Create a specific watching the film activity (see stage 3)
- Create a specific culminating activity related to the film (see stage 4) *
- Get permission from administration to use the film in the classroom *
- Get permission from students' parents/guardians that permit viewing *
- Arrange for appropriate equipment (DVD/VCR Player, LCD projector, TV, etc...) *
- Arrange classroom for viewing *

Remember:
   Film should NOT be used as a time-filler. Film should NOT be used as the lesson, but only to enhance the lesson.

Table 1.1 (Continued) *Russell Model for Using Film*

Stage 2: The Pre-viewing Stage

The pre-viewing stage is done prior to students viewing the film.
The pre-viewing stage includes the following, but is not limited to the following: (* Denotes required activities)

- Introduction of the film to students *
- Explain the purpose for viewing the film *
- Introduction of new vocabulary *
- Relate the film to student's prior knowledge *
- Relate the film to student's everyday lives *
- Relate the film to other content areas *
- Clarify any cinematic terminology (e.g. close-up, voice-over) *
- Discuss what is required during the viewing of the film *
- Discuss the culminating activity that will follow the viewing of the film *
- Discuss the background of the film *
- Collect permission slips from parents/guardians (Ideally, this should be done days prior to showing the film. Furthermore, administrative permission should be obtained prior to obtaining parent/guardian permission) *

Other Ideas for the Pre-viewing Stage

- K-W-L: What I Know, What I Want to Know, and What I Learned
- Read film reviews
- Read interviews with the star, director, producer, etc…

Table 1.1 (Continued) *Russell Model for Using Film*

Stage 3: Watching the Film Stage

Watching the film stage is where students actually view the film.
The watching the film stage includes the following: (* Denotes required activities)

- Watch the film*

Showing the entire film is appropriate when necessary, as is showing small segments or clips. Research has been shown to support both types of film use. Stopping the film occasional to highlight an important point, concept, issue, and/or scene is appropriate.

Other Ideas for Watching the Film Stage

- Have students take notes (If notes are required, the teacher must provide ample light and time for writing the notes)
- Complete a guided activity (Some films have pre-made guided activities)
- Answer questions created by the teacher

Table 1.1 (Continued) *Russell Model for Using Film*

Stage 4: The Culminating Activity Stage

The culminating activity stage is done after students have watched the film.
The culminating activity stage includes the following, but is not limited to the following: (* Denotes required activities)

- Stop the film*
- Review and discuss major points, concepts, issues, and/or scenes*
- Assess student learning (see assessment ideas below)*

Assessment Ideas

- Class discussion
- Class debate
- Rewrite the ending of the film
- Write a review of the film
- Take a test/quiz
- Complete a worksheet
- Reenactment (Have students reenact a scene from the film.
- Mock interview with the star, director, and/or producer of the film
- Have students analyze and evaluate the film.

Many of the activities that are found in the *Russell Model for Using Film* have been found to help increase student achievement. Allen (1955) found that if teachers announce a test during the pre-viewing stage that students will learn more than students who were unaware of the test prior to showing the film. Allen also found that if teachers introduce and prepare the class for a film during the pre-viewing stage, students retained more content information then students who did not receive the same introduction and preparation.

By using the *Russell Model for Using Film*, teachers will help ensure that film is used to enhance the curriculum, not as the curriculum. Furthermore, teachers will help ensure that film is used effectively and legally. The *Russell Model for Using Film* should be used as a guide; however teachers still need to make sure that all professional, ethical, and legal standards are being upheld. For more information on the legal aspects of using film in the classroom, see Chapter Two, "Legal Issues."

TWO

LEGAL ISSUES

Many teachers use film, however they are unaware of the legal issues surrounding its use. It is extremely crucial that teachers understand and follow the law, when using copyrighted materials. The two main legal issues surrounding film use in the classroom are 1) school/school district policies and regulations and 2) copyright.

School/school district policies and regulations should be upheld. Since policies and regulations change from school to school and district to district, teachers need to check with school administrators or school district administrators to obtain the policies and regulations for using film in the classroom.

As stated above, policies and regulations for using film in the classroom change from school to school and district to district. A basic policy for using film in the classroom will be similar to the following:

1) All films must be used in the classroom for instructional purposes.
2) Films with a rating of "G" may be used for instructional purposes with teacher approval and administrative permission.

3) Films with a rating of PG may be used for instructional purposes with teacher approval, administrative permission, and parent/guardian permission.
4) Films with a rating of PG-13 may be used for instructional purposes with teacher approval, administrative permission, and parent/guardian permission.
5) Films with a rating of R and/or higher cannot be shown.

Copyright laws are federal and are established by the United States Copyright Office. Section 110 (1) of Title 17 of the United States Code on Copyright and Conditions cites the following exemption for the use of copyrighted films for educational purposes:

Performance or display of a work by instructors or pupils in the course of face-to-face teaching activities of a nonprofit educational institution, in a classroom or similar place devoted to instruction, unless in the case of a motion picture or other audiovisual work, the performance, or the display of individual images, is given by means of a copy that was not lawfully made under this title, and that the person responsible for the performance knew or had reason to believe was not lawfully made (ww.copyright.gov/title17/92chap1.html#110).

Simply put, a film must be used in a non-profit educational institution, in an instructional class that is meeting face-to-face, and for educational purposes, not entertainment or recreation. As well, educators can use a film that has been rented at a video store, borrowed from a library, and/or purchased, as long as the above regulations are adhered to.

However, teachers should not make copies of films, use films as public performance, and/or make a profit from showing films. Teachers can make copies of public television programs for educational use in the classroom. This practice is covered under the fair use code of copyrighted material. What is fair use? Section 107 of Title 17 (1) of the United States Code on Copyright and Conditions explains the fair use guidelines for the use of copyrighted materials for educational purposes:

Notwithstanding the provisions of sections 106 and 106A, the fair use of a copyrighted work, including such use by reproduction in copies or phonorecords or by any other means specified by that section, for purposes such as criticism, comment, news reporting, teaching (including multiple copies for classroom use), scholarship, or research, is not an infringement of copyright. In determining whether the use made of a work in any particular case is a fair use the factors to be considered shall include—

1) the purpose and character of the use, including whether such use is of a commercial nature or is for nonprofit educational purposes;
2) the nature of the copyrighted work;
3) the amount and substantiality of the portion used in relation to the copyrighted work as a whole; and
4) the effect of the use upon the potential market for or value of the copyrighted work (www.copyright.gov/title17/92chap1.html#107).

The complete United States Code on Copyright and Conditions can be accessed via the Internet. The web address is http://www.copyright.gov/title17/.

Furthermore, to qualify as fair use, the Federal Guidelines for Off-Air Recording of Broadcast Programming for Educational Purposes (1981) should be adhered to. Those guidelines are as follows:

1) The guidelines were developed to apply only to off-air recording by nonprofit educational institutions.
2) A broadcast program may be recorded off-air simultaneously with broadcast transmission -- (including simultaneous cable re-transmission) and retained by a nonprofit educational institution for a period not to exceed the first forty-five (45) consecutive calendar days after date of recording. Upon conclusion of such retention period, all off-air recordings must be ceased or de-

stroyed immediately. "Broadcast programs" are television programs transmitted by television stations for reception by the general public without charge.

3) Off-air recordings may be used by individual teachers in the course of relevant teaching activities, and repeated once only when instructional reinforcement is necessary, in classrooms and similar places devoted to instruction within a single buildings, cluster, or campus, as well as in the homes of students receiving formalized home instruction, during the first ten (10) consecutive school days in the forty-five (45) day calendar day retention period. "School days" are school session days-- not counting weekends, holidays, vacations, examination periods, or other scheduled interruptions--within the forty-five (45) calendar day retention period.

4) Off-Air recordings may be made only at the request of and used by individual teachers, and may not be regularly recorded in anticipation of requests. No broadcast program may be recorded off-air more than once at the request of the same teacher, regardless of the number of times the program may be broadcast.

5) A limited number of copies may be reproduced from each off-air recording to meet the legitimate needs of teachers under these guidelines. Each such additional copy shall be subject to all provisions governing the original recording.

6) After the first ten (10) consecutive school days, off-air recordings may be used up to the end of the forty-five (45) calendar day retention period only for teacher evaluation purposes, i.e., to determine whether or not to include the broadcast program in the teaching curriculum, and may not be used in the recording institution for student exhibition or any other non-evaluation purpose without authorization.

7) Off-air recordings need not be used in their entirety, but the recorded programs may not be altered from their original content. Off-air recordings may not be physi-

cally or electronically combined or merged to constitute teaching anthologies or compilations.

8) All copies of off-air recordings must include the copyright notice on the broadcast programs as recorded.

9) Educational Institutions are expected to establish the appropriate control procedures to maintain the integrity of these guidelines (p. E4750-E4752).

THREE

REVIEW OF LITERATURE

Creation of Celluloid

Interested researchers have been studying what techniques are best for showing film in the classroom since film was invented. George Eastman, the founder of Kodak, created flexible celluloid in 1888/9, which was the basis for motion picture film. Then, in 1891, Thomas Edison introduced the kinetoscope, a small peephole viewer for watching short and simple motion pictures. However, only a single person could view Edison's invention.

Eastman's creation of celluloid and Edison's kinetoscope helped spawn an era of silent films. Silent films were the only available film in the early 1900's, and it was not until the 1930's that films with sound became readily available.

Brief Historical Review of Film Research in Education

The use of film in education has been prevalent since the creation of film. Researchers started looking at the effects of film on education as early as 1915. One of the first experimental studies published was "A Comparative Study of Visual Instruction in the High School" published in 1918 (Sumstine). In the years following, film use in education continued to grow as technology advanced. As film use in the classroom became more readily avail-

able, research on the effects of film use in the classroom also became more common.

In 1931, Frances Consitt completed a study on the value of
films in teaching history. Consitt (1931) concludes his study with
many extremely important findings. Below is a list of the general
effects of historical teaching with film.

- The historical film gives life to the past.
- It arouses interest and stimulates intellectual curiosity.
- It stimulates imagination.
- It corrects, clarifies, and simplifies previous knowledge.
- It portrays incidental details not found in textbooks and
  often taken for granted by the teacher.
- It aids retention
- It gives pleasure to children, which should cause history
  to be more meaningful to them (p. 431).

Wise (1939) used five high schools in Missouri to study the use
of film in the social studies classroom. He found the following
methods to be the most effective.

- Teachers should have a good introduction to the topic
  and to the film.
- Show film without stopping for discussion.
- Show the film twice (if the historical background of the
  film was not clearly explained).
- A period of discussion should follow each film.
- A post viewing written activity should take place.

The research of film in the classroom continued to be a focal
point of some academics, and from 1947-1949, 15,000 subjects
were studied at Pennsylvania State University (Carpenter, 1949).
These studies demonstrate the push to understand the effects of
film in the classroom and on learning.

Not only had the educational world discovered a powerful and
effective tool, but the U.S. military branches also started to use
film as an instructional aid. In 1947, just after World War II, the

U.S. Naval Department listed the following reasons for using film as instructional training aids, 1) to learn more, 2) to remember longer, and 3) to increase interest (Fern & Robbins, 1947).

The research dealing with film in education and the outcomes of film use in instruction, from 1918-1950 (often referred to as the comparative period), was analyzed and summarized in 1970 by Hoban and Van Ormer.

- People learn from films
- The use of effective and appropriate film results in more learning in less time and better retention of what is learned.
- Film in combination with other instructional materials are better than either alone.
- Instructional films stimulate other learning activities.
- Films facilitate thinking and problem solving.
- Films are equivalent to a good instructor in communicating facts or demonstrating procedures (Hoban & Van Ormer).

According to Wittich, film in the 1950's was known as the medium with limitless possibilities for research studies (1953).

Carpenter (1953) researched the preparation of film for instruction. The researcher reviewed, analyzed, and summarized sixty-three research reports. The following was found:

- Films with broad superficial content for general audiences are less effective than films with specified content for specific audiences.
- Films should be prepared for a specific audience and tailored to a specific audience.

Allen (1955) reviewed research on the use of film in the classroom and concluded the following:

- A teacher introduction and preparing the class for showing a film, results in a significant gain in factual content retained, compared to showing a film without introduction.

- A teacher introduction is just as important as a review of the film after showing.
- Announcing a test before showing the film results in increased learning compared to not announcing a test.
- Teacher introductions have a motivating effect.

Allen (1957) studied student participation and found that films help increase student participation. He also concluded that higher levels of participation during a film result in increased learning.

Researchers concluded that using guided activity worksheets could secure greater academic returns when showing films. Guided activity worksheets that have objective questions were found to make a significant difference in student learning. The results of the summary found that guided activity worksheets could do the following:

- Produce increased learning.
- Define the aims for viewing and help highlight the films importance.
- Present a task that eliminates the idea that films are only for entertainment.
- Highlight specific information.
- Helps make learning permanent since reading and writing also occur.
- The worksheet gives facts, so when the student is at home he can discuss it with family (Robert & Parchert, 1962). '

A national study called Project Discovery, surveyed teachers about the use of film in education. Teachers were asked: What purposes have films and filmstrips served for your teaching most of the time? Please check all that apply. Below is a list of the conclusions in order of highest approval:

- To motivate students about some new topic-97%.

- To provide students with a common experience, which would be generally unobtainable in any other way-92%.
- To provide a review or summary of information learned in other ways by the class-91%.
- To convey a set of important facts-85%.
- To develop an attitude or appreciation for some abstract idea or concept-75%.
- To provide supplementary or enrichment experiences for individual student study times-73%.
- To clarify complex ideas-68%.
- To provide an occasional break for enjoyment-68%.
- To explain a skill-58% (Eboch, 1966).

Under most conditions a motion picture, film, video or movie is the most effective tool for presenting information to be learned cognitively (Allen & Weintraub, 1968). Dale (1969) created eight general conclusions about audio-visual materials, which are:

- Heightens motivation for learning.
- Provides freshness and variety.
- Appeals to students of varied abilities.
- Encourages active participation.
- Gives needed reinforcement.
- Widens the range of student experience.
- Assures order and continuity of thought.
- Improves the effectiveness of other materials.

Greenhill (1967) concludes that era of research from 1950's-1960's was lost to the popularity of television. Television drew much attention by researchers and the emphasis on film as an instructional tool switched to television as an instructional tool.

Eight-millimeter films had become extremely popular as well as inexpensive and easy to use in the sixties and seventies. The use of 8mm films in the classroom brought on a new wave in the educational world. The use of 8mm film increased as the hardware developed. Gerlach (1970) described the 8mm as the new teaching tool because of its accessibility, economic value, and practicality.

Ken Smith the author of "Mental Hygiene" (1999) explains that between 1945 and 1970, schools around the United States were using film to teach teenagers about proper hygiene, dating etiquette, substance abuse, vandalism, and other social issues. He believes that these films were effective in teaching students, when showing films was a relatively novel classroom strategy. However, as the years went on, the use of film to teach students what the author calls "mental hygiene" was not effective.

In 1971, Maynard found that film can motivate students. He studied an inner-city class and found that using film helped engage students who usually would be inattentive.

One study looked at the effects of providing the learner with instructional objectives prior to instruction. The study concluded that presenting objectives to learners prior to watching the film allows the learner to focus on relevant material (Smith, Roberts, & Taylor, 1973).

Researchers have found that objectives provide students with a direction for learning (Duchastel & Brown, 1974). Researchers started looking at behavioral and instructional objectives in the late sixties and early seventies.

In 1979, Salomon concluded that teachers must guide students prior to showing a film. If guidance or direction is not given prior to showing the film students will not be completely engaged. Furthermore, he concludes that allowing for discussion after the film has been viewed, helps increase retention and comprehension.

Mattheisen (1989) explained that the biggest problem with using film in the classroom is finding the right film to use. "The problem has two aspects. First, a good film – one that is instructive, relevant to the course, and sensitive to historical issues – must be available. Second, we must find the film."

Wilson and Herman (1994) have created a guide for showing specific films in the history classroom. They suggest using their "unit sheet," which is a pre-made worksheet about a specific film, before showing the film. The unit sheet provides vocabulary and they believe it is vital for the teacher to review the terms before showing the film.

Fuller (1999) explains that film is an effective tool for teaching history, when teachers create "a challenging lesson plan to engage students in active analysis and interpretation."

Cantu and Warren (2003) explain that film can be effective but teachers are apprehensive to use film correctly because of time. Teaching visually takes a greater effort and demands more time.

In 2005, the Film Foundation released film curriculum for the middle grades. As well, the Film Foundation provides educators with lessons and activities for teaching students about film and history on film. Furthermore, the Film Foundation has created the national film standards to help middle graders develop literacy in moving images. The Film Foundation can be accessed at www.storyofmovies.org.

In a study of teaching practices for educating students about the Holocaust, 69% of the teachers reported that they use some type of film/movie to teach this subject matter. A total of 327 teachers from across the United States were surveyed. The method of using film to teach about the Holocaust and the method using first hand accounts of the Holocaust were tied for the number one method teachers used to teach the Holocaust (Donnelly, 2006).

In a national survey of social studies teachers conducted in 2006, 63% of eight grade teachers reported using some type of video-based activity in last social studies class they taught (Leming, Ellington, & Schug).

Conclusion

In summary, the related research reveals an investigation into the role film has played in education. The way film has been used in the classroom, according to the research creates a solid foundation for the study described in chapter four, "Research Study." Plus, it provideˢ a rationale for using film in the classroom. Among the research, film was found to be effective when used in the classroom. Understanding the benefits of film use and the procedures for using film in the classroom will increase appropriate film use by teachers. Furthermore, the research discussed in this chapter is by no means a comprehensive review of all the research on film in education. Instead, this chapter is a look at the historical journey of film use in education.

FOUR

RESEARCH STUDY

Purpose of Study

The purpose of this study was to examine social studies teachers' practices for using film in the classroom. This study used three separate variables to determine three separate outcomes.

1) Whether graduating from a teacher preparation program affects how teachers use film in the social studies classroom.
2) Whether having continuing contract affects how teachers use film in the social studies classroom.
3) Whether years of teaching experience affects how teachers use film in the social studies classroom.

In the three statements above, the dependent variables of this study were defined. The independent variable in this study is the mean score on *the use of film survey/questionnaire* (see Appendix).

Studying how social studies teachers use film in the classroom will help determine, if teachers are using film to enhance instruction and learning in a lesson, if the proper rules and regulations are being followed, and/or if film is being used as a reward or time-filler. More specifically, the objectives of this study are to provide evidence for the following research problems:

1) Do social studies teachers follow the recommended guidelines for showing a film?
2) Do social studies teachers obtain administrative and parental permission before showing a film?

Historians have found that film images impact and influence a person's perspective of history (O'Connor & Jackson, 1988), thus it is important to study how social studies teachers are using film. Furthermore, historians have also found that history on film can be an accurate interpretation of history (Rosenstone, 1995) and that film can bring students closer to the people and events that they are studying (Matz & Pingatore, 2005).

Discovering whether social studies teachers are using the recommended guidelines when using film in the classroom and whether teachers who graduate from a teacher preparation program or teachers who have continuing contract or teachers who have more years of teaching experience are the teachers who are more likely to use the recommended guidelines, can help improve the process of teaching with film. Moreover, it can insure that teachers are maximizing instructional time, thus helping to insure that students have ample opportunities to improve academic achievement.

Variables

The dependent variable in this study is *the use of film survey/questionnaire* (see Appendix). A mean score will be determined from questions 1-20. This will determine how secondary social studies teachers use film in the classroom. Overall, questions 1-20 ask how responsibly social studies teachers use film in the classroom.

The independent variables in this study are as follows:

1) Whether the teachers graduated from a teacher preparation program
2) Whether teachers have continuing contract
3) Years of teaching experience

The independent variables were chosen for various reasons. Variable one was chosen because currently more teachers are being hired without any teacher training. An enormous amount of teachers in public schools have no educational background. This is due to the need for teachers; schools are forced to hire teachers with no teaching experience and/or teacher training. These teachers take an alternative route to becoming certified. This variable will help determine if teacher preparation programs and/or alternative certification programs are producing teachers who effectively use film in the classroom.

Variable two was chosen because many believe that once a teacher has continuing contract the quality of work decreases, since they have a higher level of job security. This will bring to question whether teachers stop trying to be effective once they have continuing contract.

Variable three was chosen because many believe that an old dog is unable to learn new tricks. For the most part teaching with film is not new, but it is utilized more often in today's classrooms, compared to years prior. This is because of advances in technology. In the past it was a major ordeal to get a filmstrip and show it in class. Now, it is relatively easy to rent a DVD/ VHS and press play. This variable will show that veteran teachers can use film and bring to question whether only young teachers use technology in the classroom.

Hypotheses

The outcome of this research will determine how social studies teachers use film in the classroom and what variables affect how film is used. The following alternative hypotheses were postulated for this study.

1) H1: Classroom social studies teachers who graduated from a teacher preparation program are more likely to follow the recommended guidelines for showing a film in the social studies classroom then social studies teachers who did not graduate from a teacher preparation program.

2) H1: Classroom social studies teachers who have more years of teaching experience are more likely to follow the recommended guidelines for showing a film in the social studies classroom then social studies teachers with less years of experience.

3) H1: Classroom social studies teachers who have continuing contract are more likely to follow the recommended guidelines for showing a film in the social studies classroom then social studies teachers who do not have continuing contract.

Since the majority of social studies teachers will use film in the social studies classroom, it is extremely important to understand whether film is being incorporated into the curriculum appropriately. Determining how film is being used in the social studies classroom and whether social studies teachers are following recommended guidelines will help strengthen teacher preparation programs. If the alternative hypotheses are supported this information is helpful, and once presented, will help encourage future teachers to use recognized and research-based guidelines when incorporating film into the social studies classroom. Furthermore, the results of this study will highlight specific needs that must be addressed to enable teachers, who did not graduate from a teacher preparation program and are going through an alternative certification program, with the recommended guidelines for using film in the social studies classroom.

For statistical purposes, all hypotheses postulated in this study assume the null form of no significant difference.

Participants

Roughly two hundred secondary social studies teachers in Florida were given the opportunity to participate in this study. A total of seventy teachers chose to participate in the study; a return rate of 35%. For privacy purposes, the names of participants, schools, and school districts will not be revealed. The sample population of the study consisted of secondary (grades 6-12) social studies teachers who chose to participate in this study, which totaled seventy (n=70).

The seventy teachers were from two separate school districts that represent rural, suburban, and urban populations. The diverse population of teachers not only provides ethnic diversity, but also academic and cultural diversity. The participants of this study had varying demographics. (see Table 4.1).

Table 4.1 Breakdown of Demographics

*(Denotes that all teachers did not report the specific data)

Demographic		
Sex*	Male=37	Female=32
Race	Hispanic/Latino/a=3 White=59	Black=6 Other=2
Graduates of a Teacher Preparation Program	Yes=48	No=22 (Alternative Certification)
Had Continuing Contract	Yes=55 Unsure=5	No=15
Years of Teaching Experience*	0-4 Years=18 10 or More Years=26	5-9 Years=20

Materials

The only material that was used to complete this study was *the use of film survey/questionnaire* (see Appendix) that was created to measure how teachers use film. It was sent to participants via email.

Instrument

This study utilized a questionnaire/survey method to obtain information about whether teaching experience, graduating from a teacher preparation program, and/or having continuing contract affects the use of film by social studies teachers. The information that was gathered was used to draw inferences concerning the use of film by social studies teachers. The survey used a continuous interval scale similar to the Likert scale; this "provides continuous response options to questions with assumed equal distances between options" (Creswell, p. 168). The questionnaire was administered in a pilot study at a public school in Florida.

Pilot Study

Prior to the questionnaire/survey being administered, a pilot test was done to determine the reliability of the items on the questionnaire/survey. Prior to testing the reliability of the questionnaire, the validity was tested in a graduate level survey research design course at a major research university in Florida. Over twenty-five graduate students as well as a tenured professor checked the face, criterion-related, construct, and content validity of the instrument. Once the validity was checked, the pilot test was administered at a public school in Florida to seven secondary social studies teachers. These seven teachers were excluded from the research group.

To test the reliability of the survey instrument, Cronbach's Alpha was used to determine the reliability coefficient. Cronbach's Alpha calculates a reliability coefficient that describes the degree to which scores on a measure represent something other than measurement error (Glass & Hopkins, 1996). The data was first coded (see Table 4.3) and then input into Statistical Package for the Social Sciences (SPSS). Using SPSS to analyze the data, a Cronbach's Alpha was run and the pilot study concluded a Cronbach Alpha reliability coefficient score of .724 (see table 4.2). According to Santos (1999) anything over a .7 is considered an acceptable reliability coefficient.

Table 4.2 Cronbach's Alpha Reliability Statistics

Cronbach's Alpha	Cronbach's Alpha Based on Standardized Items	N of Items
.724	.768	20

Survey Design

This comparison study utilized a questionnaire/survey. The questionnaire/survey was administered via email to all participants and was used to measure how social studies teachers use film in the secondary classroom.

Survey research design was used for this study to help predict if graduating from a teacher preparation program, having continuing contract, and/or years of teaching experience has an effect on how secondary social studies teachers use film in classroom. The statistical data that was gathered offered quantifiable findings.

Dependent Variable

The dependent variable in this study is the twenty-question *the use of film survey/questionnaire* (see Appendix). This will determine how secondary social studies teachers use film in the classroom. Refer to Table 4.3 Coding of Data, to see how the data was coded.

Independent Variables

The independent variables in this study are:

1) Whether the teachers graduated from a teacher preparation program (Data was coded as follows: Yes=1, No=2).

2) Whether teachers have continuing contract (Data was coded as follows: Yes=1, No=2).
3) The years of teaching experience a teacher has (Data was coded as follows: 0-4 Years=1, 5-9 Years=2, 10 or More Years=3).

Table 4.3 Coding of Data

Almost all of the time or All the time	More than half of the time	Half of the time	Less than half of the time	Very little of the time or Never
1	2	3	4	5

Procedures

Once the voluntary survey was completed the data was analyzed. Prior to administering the survey, permission was obtained from the appropriate authorities (human subject's board, school districts, & principals). Once permission was obtained a mass email to each individual teacher was sent. The email also served as the informed consent form.

Statistical Analysis

The Statistical Package for the Social Sciences (SPSS) software was utilized to analyze the data. Analysis of Variance (ANOVA) was done to test each hypothesis. Analysis of Variance computed the mean scores of each of the following groups of the respondents to be compared.

1) Graduates compared to non-graduates of teacher preparation programs.
2) Teachers who have continuing contract compared to teachers who do not have continuing contract.
3) Comparing teachers with 0-4 years, 5-9 years, and 10 or more years of teaching experience.

   Testing the null hypothesis (Ho) allowed a decision to be made whether to reject or accept Ho for each hypothesis. The null hypotheses are as follows:

Null Hypothesis 1
   Ho: Classroom social studies teachers who graduated from a teacher preparation program are just as likely to follow the recommended guidelines for showing a film in the social studies classroom as social studies teachers who did not graduate from a teacher preparation program.

Null Hypothesis 2:
   Ho: Classroom social studies teachers who have more years of teaching experience are just as likely to follow the recommended guidelines for showing a film in the social studies classroom as social studies teachers with less years of experience.

Null Hypothesis 3:
   Ho: Classroom social studies teachers who have continuing contract are just as likely to follow the recommended guidelines for showing a film in the social studies classroom as social studies teachers who do not have continuing contract.

FIVE

RESULTS OF STUDY

Following the procedures outlined in chapter four, "Research Study", data from *the use of film survey/questionnaire* was utilized to determine if graduating from a teacher preparation program enhances a social studies teacher's ability to use recommended strategies when showing film in the classroom. *The use of film survey/questionnaire* also provided data to determine if teaching experience had an affect on how social studies teachers use film, as well as, if having continuing contract affects how social studies teachers use film in the classroom.

Seventy public school social studies teachers from Florida completed *the use of film survey/questionnaire*. The survey was sent to social studies teachers in Florida in fall of 2005 via email. Every social studies teacher who chose to participate had one calendar month to complete the survey. After one-month, a total of seventy social studies teachers had participated in the study.

Each hypothesis will be presented separately. The results will consist of a restatement of the hypothesis, an overview of the analysis used, and the decision in regards to the hypothesis. A detailed discussion pertaining to each hypothesis will be presented in chapter six, "Discussion of Results."

Furthermore, the detailed results of the participant's responses to each question on the survey/questionnaire will be provided.

Hypothesis One
Alternative Hypothesis:

H1: Classroom social studies teachers who graduated from a teacher preparation program are more likely to follow the recommended guidelines for showing a film in the social studies classroom then social studies teachers who did not graduate from a teacher preparation program.

Null Hypothesis:

Ho: Classroom social studies teachers who graduated from a teacher preparation program are just as likely to follow the recommended guidelines for showing a film in the social studies classroom as social studies teachers who did not graduate from a teacher preparation program.

Analysis/Decision

The differences between the mean scores of *the use of film survey/questionnaire* were compared by analysis of variance (ANOVA). The data concluded that there is a significant difference (P-Value = .000250) between graduates of a teacher preparation program (mean = 2.2529) compared to non-graduates of a teacher preparation program (mean = 2.8258) and how they use film in the social studies classroom (see Tables 5.1 & 5.2). Therefore the null hypothesis (stated above) was rejected and the alternative hypothesis (stated above) was accepted.

Table 5.1 Descriptive Statistics for Hypothesis One (Teacher Preparation Program)

	N	Mean	Standard Deviation	Standard Error	95% Confidence Interval for Mean		Minimum	Maximum
					Lower Bound	Upper Bound		
Yes	48	2.2529	.55805	.08055	2.0909	2.4150	1.15	3.80
No	22	2.8258	.61263	.13061	2.5541	3.0974	1.75	3.90
Total	70	2.4330	.63094	.07541	2.2825	2.5834	1.15	3.90

Table 5.2 ANOVA for Hypothesis One (Teacher Preparation Program)

	Sum of Squares	df	Mean Square	F	Sig.
Between Groups	4.950	1	4.950	14.948	.000250
Within Groups	22.518	68	.331		
Total	27.468	69			

*This data is significant at .05

Coding:
Yes (1.0) = Teacher Preparation Graduate
No (2.0) = Non-Teacher Preparation Graduate

Hypothesis Two
Alternative Hypothesis:
   H1: Classroom social studies teachers who have more years of teaching experience are more likely to follow the recommended guidelines for showing a film in the social studies classroom then social studies teachers with less years of experience.

Null Hypothesis:
   Ho: Classroom social studies teachers who have more years of teaching experience are just as likely to follow the recommended guidelines for showing a film in the social studies classroom as social studies teachers who have less years of experience.

Analysis/Decision
   The differences between the mean scores of *the use of film survey/questionnaire* were compared by analysis of variance (ANOVA). The data concluded that there is a significant difference (P-Value = .027) between social studies teachers with more teaching experience compared to social studies teachers with less teaching experience and how they use film in the social studies classroom (see Tables 5.3 & 5.4). Therefore the null hypothesis (stated above) was rejected and the alternative hypothesis (stated above) was accepted.

Table 5.3 Descriptive Statistics for Hypothesis Two (Years of Teaching Experience)

Years of Experience	N	Mean	Standard Deviation	Standard Error	95% Confidence Interval for Mean		Minimum	Maximum
					Lower Bound	Upper Bound		
0-4 Years	18	2.6731	.72249	.17029	2.3139	3.0324	1.40	3.85
5-9 Years	20	2.5613	.63939	.14297	2.2621	2.8606	1.74	3.90
10 or More	26	2.1884	.51364	.10073	1.9809	2.3959	1.15	3.25
Total	64	2.4413	.64434	.08054	2.2803	2.6022	1.15	3.90

Table 5.4 ANOVA for Hypothesis Two (Years of Teaching Experience)

	Sum of Squares	df	Mean Square	F	Sig.
Between Groups	2.919	2	1.459	3.831	.027
Within Groups	23.237	61	.381		
Total	26.156	63			

* This data is significant at .05

Coding:
1.0 = 0-4 Years of Teaching Experience
2.0 = 5-9 Years of Teaching Experience
3.0 = 10 or More Years of Teaching Experience

After the data concluded that there was a significant difference, a Post Hoc Test was done to examine the exact differences (See Table 5.5).

The data in Table 5.5 concludes that social studies teachers with ten or more years of teaching experience reportedly use film significantly different (p-Value = .013) from social studies teachers with zero to four years of experience.

The data also concludes that social studies teachers with ten or more years of teaching experience use film significantly different (p-Value = .047) from social studies teachers with five to nine years of teaching experience.

There is no significant difference between social studies teachers who have zero to four years of teaching experience and social studies teachers who have five to nine years of teaching experience.

Table 5.5 Multiple Comparisons (Post Hoc Test) for Hypothesis Two (Years of Teaching Experience)

(I) Teaching Experience	(J) Teaching Experience	Mean Difference (I-J)	Standard Error	Sig.	95% Confidence Interval	
					Lower Bound	Upper Bound
0-4 Years	5-9 Years	.11183	.20052	.579	-.2891	.5128
	10 or More Years	.48475	.18925	.013	.1063	.8632
5-9 Years	0-4 Years	-.11183	.20052	.579	-.5128	.2891
	10 or More Years	.37292	.18357	.047	.0059	.7400
10 or More Years	0-4 Years	-.48475	.18925	.013	-.8632	-.1063
	5-9 Years	-.37292	.18357	.047	-.7400	-.0059

* The mean difference is significant at the .05 level.

Hypothesis Three

Alternative Hypothesis:

H1: Classroom social studies teachers who have continuing contract are more likely to follow the recommended guidelines for showing a film in the social studies classroom then social studies teachers who do not have continuing contract.

Null Hypothesis:

Ho: Classroom social studies teachers who have continuing contract are just as likely to follow the recommended guidelines for showing a film in the social studies classroom as social studies teachers who do not have continuing contract.

Analysis/Decision

The differences between the mean scores of *the use of film survey/questionnaire* were compared by analysis of variance (ANOVA). The data concluded that there is no significant difference (P-Value = .188) between social studies teachers with continuing contract (mean = 2.3894) compared to social studies teachers without continuing contract (mean = 2.4125) and how they use film in the social studies classroom (see Tables 5.6 & 5.7). Therefore the null hypothesis (stated above) was accepted.

Table 5.6 ANOVA for Hypothesis Three (Continuing Contract)

	Sum of Squares	df	Mean Square	F	Sig.
Between Groups	1.336	2	.668	1.713	.188
Within Groups	26.132	67	.390		
Total	27.468	69			

* This data is significant at .05

Coding:

Yes (1.0) = Teachers with Continuing Contract

No (2.0) = Teachers without Continuing Contract

Unsure (3.0) = Teachers who are unsure if they have Continuing Contract.

Table 5.7 Descriptive Statistics for Hypothesis Three (Continuing Contract)

	N	Mean	Standard Deviation	Standard Error	95% Confidence Interval for Mean		Minimum	Maximum
					Lower Bound	Upper Bound		
Yes	50	2.3894	.62562	.08848	2.2116	2.5672	1.15	3.90
No	15	2.4125	.67241	.17362	2.0401	2.7848	1.40	3.80
Unsure	5	2.9300	.39465	.17649	2.4400	3.4200	2.25	3.25
Total	70	2.4330	.63094	.07541	2.2825	2.5834	1.15	3.90

Survey/Questionnaire Responses

The majority of participants answered all twenty questions on the survey/questionnaire. To see the detailed report of how the participants responded to each question see Table 5.8.

Table 5.8 Survey/Questionnaire Responses

*Data is presented in percentages

Film-Related Activities How Often Do You...	Al-most all of the time or All the time	More than half of the time	Half of the time	Less than half of the time	Very little of the time or Never
1. Give a verbal introduction to the film?	100.	0	0	0	0
2. Mention ideas, situations, or events that students should focus on while viewing?	78.6	12.9	4.3	2.9	1.4
3. Give some type of pre-viewing activity?	35.7	21.4	18.6	11.4	12.9
4. Have students complete some type of activity while watching the film?	48.6	22.9	1.4	12.9	14.3
5. Give a culminating activity related to the film?	54.3	18.6	11.4	7.1	5.7
6. Give a verbal summary of the film after it is shown?	62.9	11.4	14.3	8.6	2.9
7. Develop your own activities to accompany the film?	51.4	20.	10.	12.9	4.3
8. Include items on tests, which are derived from the film?	38.6	17.1	14.3	20.	10.
9. Show a film when you have a substitute teacher?	7.1	15.7	20.	12.9	42.9
10. Show a film as a reward?	7.1	8.6	10.	15.7	57.1
11. View the film prior to using it in the classroom?	74.3	12.9	5.7	4.3	2.9
12. Hold a class discussion about the film?	55.7	18.6	14.3	10.	1.4
13. Allow for a question & answer session after the watching a film?	51.4	25.7	10.	8.6	2.9
14. Get permission from school administration before showing a film?	30.	11.4	8.9	15.7	31.4
15. Get parental permission before showing a film?	28.6	15.3	11.4	15.7	27.1
16. Show the entire film with out stopping?	5.7	21.4	18.6	21.4	32.9
17. Stop the film periodically to highlight different points?	27.1	35.7	18.6	11.4	7.1
18. Only show small segments or clips from a film?	14.3	22.9	22.9	18.6	20.
19. Use written assessments related to the film for grading?	32.9	17.1	20.	10.	18.6
20. Use observation or non-written assessment related to the film for grading?	20.	17.1	22.9	14.3	25.7

SIX

DISCUSSION OF RESULTS

This study was designed to investigate whether certain factors affect how social studies teachers use film in the classroom. More specifically, this study attempted to determine if variables such as graduating from a teacher preparation program, years of teaching experience, and having continuing contract correlates with how social studies teachers use film in the social studies classroom.

Each hypothesis will be discussed separately. After a discussion of each hypothesis, a section detailing the recommendations from the data that was concluded will be made. Following the recommendations section, limitations, and a summary will be presented.

Hypothesis One

The results of the first hypothesis concluded that social studies teachers who graduated from a teacher preparation program are more likely to use the recommended strategies for using film in the social studies classroom.

This conclusion is pertinent, because currently in the state of Florida, a teacher does not need to graduate from a teacher preparation program to teach in the public school system. Teachers can become alternatively certified. To become alternatively certified, teachers need a bachelor's degree in the content area they want to teach and they must take and pass a content examination. This will enable them to receive a three-year temporary certificate. To receive a professional certificate and be allowed to continue teaching after the three-year temporary certificate expires, the teacher needs to successfully complete courses set forth by the state. The course work is often much less than what is required by teacher preparation programs. Therefore this study concludes that alternative certification programs could possibly be lacking in providing teachers with important and significant instructional strategies for incorporating film into the social studies classroom, at least as reflected by teaching practices. Furthermore, only 70% of the teachers reported that they had received some type of formal education/training on using film in the classroom, but 100% reported that they use film at least once a month. As well, 51% reported using film at least 2-3 times a month, some even reported using film 4-5 times a month or six or more times a month.

One example that demonstrates the importance of teachers knowing and using recommended strategies is the practice of obtaining permission from the administration and parents, prior to showing a film. This practice is classified under the preparation stage of the *Russell Model for Using Film.* Out of the seventy teachers, on average, permission was obtained from administration and parents about half the time. This data is extremely terrifying.

In 2003, a second year teacher in Fort Pierce, Florida was suspended for showing the R-rated version of Dracula to his class. The assistant principal was quoted saying, "although the teacher did not show any nudity or parts of the movie that prompted the R rating, he should have sought approval before showing any movie rated anything other than G" (Associated Press, 2003).

In 2004, a middle school teacher was put on administrative leave for showing an inappropriate video. Although the Public Broadcasting System had approved the video for middle school aged children, parents felt that it was not appropriate (Associated Press, 2004).

Both of these incidents could have been avoided if the teachers would have obtained permission from the administration and parents. Obtaining permission is an activity that should take place in the preparation stage, according to the *Russell Model for Using*

Film. Teachers should first seek approval from the administration and then seek approval from parents. The day of the film (ideally days before), teachers should collect permission slips prior to watching the film. Furthermore, incidents like these are embarrassing for the teacher, school, and school district.

If alternative certification programs are lacking in providing social studies teachers with pertinent instructional strategies for using film in the classroom, alternatively certified teachers are providing a below par level of instruction and delivery of the content.

The goal of this study is to use this data to increase instruction about using film in the classroom in teacher preparation programs and in alternative certification programs.

Teaching pre-service teachers, as well as classroom teachers (who did not graduate from a teacher preparation program) the recommended guidelines for using film in the social studies classroom, will help enhance the effectiveness of classroom instruction and as a side issue, possibly help prevent an embarrassing legal issue dealing with film in the classroom.

Hypothesis Two

The results of the second hypothesis concluded that the more teaching experience a social studies teacher has the more likely he/she will use the research-based strategies for using film in the social studies classroom, as explained in the *Russell Model for Using Film.* Again, the stages of the model are as follows:

Russell Model for Using Film
1.   The Preparation Stage
2.   The Pre-Viewing Stage
3.   Watch the Film Stage
4.   The Culminating Activity Stage

For more information, refer to Table 1.1 in chapter one, "Introduction." Despite the fact that these recommended strategies are common, the research finds that teachers still need instruction. The researcher can only predict that these teachers use film more appropriately because they have been in the system longer. Thus, they have had more opportunities to learn the recommended strategies for using film in the classroom, from mentor/other teachers, administrators, teacher in-services', peer-reviewed articles, and/or professional conferences.

Determining if teaching experience affected film use in the social studies classroom is important because many schools place new teachers with a mentor teacher. However, Mullinix (2002) found that finding and retaining meaningful mentor teachers is difficult. Furthermore, new teachers/inexperienced teachers find it difficult to take a mentor teacher seriously if the mentor is not conscientious. The concept of mentoring has lost its flare and many of the mentors that the researcher had as a new teacher where reluctant to provide any useful teaching tips.

The findings of this study will hopefully encourage schools and school districts to set-up mentoring programs. Furthermore, for districts to set-up a mentoring program with some type of accountability and possibly compensation (of some sort) for the mentors. Hopefully, this will encourage mentors to offer authentic and meaningful information to less experienced teachers.

Hypothesis Three

The results of the third hypothesis concluded that there is no significant difference in how social studies teachers with continuing contract compared to social studies teachers without continuing contract use film in the classroom. This data has led to the following; although this data concludes that there is not a significant difference between social studies teachers with continuing contract and social studies teachers without continuing contract, it does not mean that teachers improve instruction once continuing contract is obtained. Furthermore, just because a teacher has continuing contract does not mean he/she cannot be disciplined for using film inappropriately. Having continuing contract does not give social studies teacher's immunity if film was used ineffectively or as a side issue, illegally.

Although the data concluded no significant difference, the results are still important. Schools, school districts, teacher preparation programs, and alternative certification programs need to discuss the teaching ethics and legal rights of teachers who have and do not have continuing contract.

Recommendations

It is recommended that teacher preparation programs continue teaching appropriate film use and that alternative certification programs start incorporating teaching with film into their program.

Furthermore, support groups should be created in schools to help make teachers aware of appropriate instructional strategies, which include the use of film.

To the extent of teachers who do not use film appropriately, school districts should create guidelines for using film in the classroom and/or provide every teacher with a copy of this book. School districts should provide periodic in-service training that deals with using film in the classroom.

Plus, it is recommended that mentoring programs be established in schools and school districts. More experienced teachers should mentor less experienced teachers in the ways of appropriate film use in the social studies classroom. A mentoring program with some type of accountability and possibly compensation (of some sort) for the mentors would be optimal. Hopefully, this will encourage mentors to offer authentic and meaningful information to less experienced teachers.

Limitations

To the degree that the seventy public social studies teachers in Florida are representative of the social studies teachers in the state of Florida, the results from this study can be generalized to that population. Thus, allowing for predictions to be made based on the results.

Making generalizations or predictions about social studies teachers at the national or international level would be a stretch. These data would not support such a claim. To make such a generalization or prediction, the study would need to be larger and include social studies teachers from all across the nation or world. However, Florida is not the only state with these problems. Many other states (e.g. Georgia, Mississippi, & California) have alternative certification routes for recruiting classroom teachers. Furthermore, others state can predict that Florida is having these problems; they most likely are having the same or similar problems.

Summary

In sum, social studies teacher use film in the classroom, as do most all teachers. The use of film to enhance the curriculum is an extremely effective strategy, when used appropriately. How they use film is heavily based upon ones individual experiences. However, there are many different variables that could affect how a social studies teacher uses film in the social studies classroom. This study defines two variables (graduating from a teacher preparation program and years of teaching experience) affecting how social studies teachers use film.

The overall conclusion of the data collected is that teacher preparation programs and years of teaching experience do affect whether social studies teachers use the recommended strategies for showing film in the social studies classroom. Therefore, school districts, schools, alternative certification programs, and teacher preparation programs should incorporate the recommended strategies for using film in the classroom into their respective areas.

SEVEN

CONCLUSION

As educational literature suggests, it is extremely appropriate to review what has been covered. Reviewing provides the opportunity for clarification, as well as a reiteration of the important topics and points discussed. The main topics and points discussed throughout this book will be revisited.

As stated in chapter one, "Introduction" film can be a double-edged sword depending on how it is used in the classroom. When used as a time-filler, film loses its educational power and is seen as a waste. However, when used effectively to enhance the curriculum, the benefits of film are numerous. To enable the latter to occur, the *Russell Model for Using Film* (see Table 1.1) should be used. The model can help ensure that film is used appropriately and effectively. Although the model is research-based and has been found to be effective, it does not protect teachers from legal issues. Teachers need to be responsible and make sure that when using the model, that local, state, and national laws/policies are being upheld.

As stated in chapter three, "Review of Literature", educators have been finding ways to incorporate film into the K-12 curriculum since the creation of film. Based on the research described in chapter three, it is obvious that using film has its academic advantages. Film can improve achievement, understanding, attitude, perception of school, and perception of the subject area, for which the film is being incorporated.

As stated in chapters four, five, and six there are specific variables that may affect how film is used in the social studies classroom. The research study looked at three different variables:

1) Whether graduating from a teacher preparation program affects how teachers use film in the social studies classroom.
2) Whether having continuing contract affects how teachers use film in the social studies classroom.
3) Whether years of teaching experience affects how teachers use film in the social studies classroom.

After testing the hypothesis using an Analysis of Variance (ANOVA), it was determined that there was a significant difference of how film is used between, graduates and non-graduates of a teacher preparation program. As well, there was a significant difference between teachers who have more teaching experience compared to teachers with less teaching experience. It was determined that there was no significant difference between teachers with continuing contract and teachers without continuing contract.

These findings are important, because in Florida and in many other states, teachers are not required to be graduates of a teacher preparation program to be certified. Meaning that alternative certification programs need to incorporate appropriate film use into the training, and teacher preparation programs need to continue film education. As well, meaningful mentorship's need to be established in schools and school districts to help ensure that less experienced teachers are being mentored in appropriate film use.

In sum, film has been found to be an effective tool for enhancing the curriculum. However, film is a serious educational tool and needs to be used as such. Using film as a time-filler is inappropriate. Teachers need to be trained in proper film use, whether in teacher preparation programs, alternative certification programs, training session, or via a mentor. Since most teachers use film in the classroom, schools, school districts, and states departments of education need to look at ensuring appropriate film use by teachers.

APPENDIX

Background Information
1. How many full school years (August-May) have you been teaching secondary (Grades 6-12) social studies? ____

2. Do you have Continuing Contract?
    ____YES   ____NO   ____UNSURE

3. Please, place an "X" next to the highest degree you have received as of today.
    ____ Bachelor's   ____ Master's
    ____ Specialist   ____ Doctorate
    ____ Other - Please Explain_____

4. Did you graduate from a teacher preparation program?
    ____YES   ____NO   ____UNSURE

5. Are you?
    ____ Male   ____ Female

6. How do you describe yourself?
    ____ White – Not Hispanic   ____ Black – Not Hispanic
    ____ Hispanic or Latino/a   ____ Asian or Pacific Islander
    ____ American Indian or Alaskan Native ____ Other

7. Have you had any formal education on using film in the classroom?
    ____YES   ____NO   ____UNSURE

8. How often do you use film in your classroom?
    ____Once a month or less   ____Two-Three times a month
    ____Four-Five times a month   ____Six or more times a month

9. Do you hold a Professional Teaching Certificate in your field?
    ____YES   ____NO   ____UNSURE

Appendix

The Use of Film Survey/Questionnaire

Place an "X" in the column that indicates the frequency with which you engage in the following activities when using film in the classroom.

Film-Related Activities How Often Do You...	Al-most all of the time or All the time	More than half of the time	Half of the time	Less than half of the time	Very little of the time or Never
1. Give a verbal introduction to the film?					
2. Mention ideas, situations, or events that students should focus on while viewing?					
3. Give some type of pre-viewing activity?					
4. Have students complete some type of activity while watching the film?					
5. Give a culminating activity related to the film?					
6. Give a verbal summary of the film after it is shown?					
7. Develop your own activities to accompany the film?					
8. Include items on tests, which are derived from the film?					
9. Show a film when you have a substitute teacher?					
10. Show a film as a reward?					
11. View the film prior to using it in the classroom?					
12. Hold a class discussion about the film?					
13. Allow for a question & answer session after the watching a film?					
14. Get permission from school administration before showing a film?					
15. Get parental permission before showing a film?					
16. Show the entire film with out stopping?					
17. Stop the film periodically to highlight different points?					
18. Only show small segments or clips from a film?					
19. Use written assessments related to the film for grading?					
20. Use observation or non-written assessment related to the film for grading?					

REFERENCES

Allen, M. (2005). 'It is as it was': Feature films in the history classroom. *The Social Studies, 96 (2),* 61-67.

Allen, W. (1955). Research on film use: student preparation. *AV Communication Review, 5,* 423-450.

———. (1957). Research on film use: class preparation. *AV Communication Review, 3,* 183-195.

Allen, W. & Weintraub, R. (1968). *The motion of variables in film presentations* (Final Report). Los Angeles, CA: University of Southern California. (ERIC Document Reproduction Service No. ED027750).

Associated Press. (2003). Teacher Suspended for Showing R-Movie Excerpt. *CNN News.* Retrieved November 7, 2005, from the World Wide Web: http://www.cnn.com/2003/EDUCATION/04/24/class.movie.ap

———. (2004). Teacher Suspended for Showing Eighth-graders "Inappropriate" Video. *KUTV.* Retrieved November 7, 2005, from the World Wide Web: http://kutv.com/topstories/local_story_127131818.html

Cantu, D.A. & Warren, W.J., (2003). *Teaching history in the digital classroom.* Armonk, NY: M.E. Sharpe.

Carpenter, C. (Director). (1949). *General summary of trends of results: The instructional film research program 1947-1949.* (Instructional Film Research Program). Pennsylvania State University.

Carpenter, C. (1953). A theoretical orientation for instructional film research. *AV Communication Review, 1,* 38-52.

Consitt, F. (1931). *The values of films in history teaching.* London, England: G. Bell and Sons, Ltd.

Creswell, J. (2005) *Educational research: planning, conducting, and evaluating quantitative and qualitative research.* Upper Saddle River, NJ: Pearson Education, Inc...

Dale, E. (1969). *Audiovisual methods in teaching.* New York, NY: Holt, Rinehart, and Winston, Inc...

Donnelly, M. (2006). Educating students about the Holocaust: A survey of teaching practices. *Social Education.* 70(1): 51-54.

Driscoll, M.P. (2000). *Psychology of learning for instruction.* Needham Heights, MA: Allyn & Bacon.

Duchastel, P. & Brown, B. (1974). Incidental and relevant learning with instructional objectives. *Journal of Psychology,* 66(4): 481-185.

Eboch, S. (1966). *Implementation of research strategies and tactics for demonstration of news media* (Final Report, Project NO. 5-0264). Columbus, OH: The Ohio State University. (ERIC Document Reproduction Service No. ED012374).

Engle, S.H. (2003). Decision-making: The heart of social studies instruction. *The Social Studies, (94) 1*: 7-10 (Reprinted with permission from *Social Education, 27 (4),* November. P. 301-304.)

Fern, G. & Robbins, E. (1947). *Teaching with films.* Milwaukee, WI: The Bruce Publishing Company.

Film Foundation. (2005). The Film Foundation. Retrieved October 21, 2006, from the World Wide Web: http://www.storyofmovies.org.

Fuller, K.H. (1999). Lessons from the screen: Film and video in the classroom. *Perspectives, 37(4).* Retrieved November 1, 2006, from the World Wide Web: http://www.historians.org/perspectives/issues/1999/9904/99 04FIL3.CFM

Gerlach, V. (1970). "Why 8mm?" *The Instructor.* January, 99.

Glass, G.V. & Hopkins, K.D. (1996). *Statistical Methods in Education and Psychology.* Boston, MA: Allyn and Bacon.

Greenhill, L. (1967). Introduction in Reid, E. & MacLennan, D. *Research in instructional television and film.* Washington DC: U.S. Department of Health, Education, and Welfare.

Hoban, C. & Van Ormer, E. (1970). *Instructional film research 1918-1950.* New York, NY: Arno Press & The New York Times.

Kaiser Family Foundation. (1999). *Kids and media @ the new millennium.* National Public Study. Retrieved June 21, 2006, from the World Wide Web: Http://www.kff.org/content/1999/1535/

Lankford, M. (1992). *Films for learning, thinking, and doing.* Englewood, CO: Libraries Unlimited, Inc...

Leming, J., Ellington, L., & Schug, M. (2006). The state of social studies: A national random survey of elementary and middle school social studies teachers. *Social Education.* 70(5): 322-327.

Levine, H. (1937). A critique of the educational film. *The Educational Screen,* January, 13-14.

Mattheisen, D. (1989). Finding the right film for the history classroom. *Perspectives, 27(9).* Retrieved November 1, 2006, from the World Wide Web: http://www.historians.org/perspectives/issues/1989/8912/8912TEC.cfm

Matz, K.A. & Pingatore, L.L. (2005). Reel to reel: Teaching the twentieth century with classic Hollywood films. *Social Education, 69(4),* 189-192.

Maynard, R. (1971). *The celluloid curriculum: how to use movies in the classroom.* New York, NY: Hayden Book Company.

Mullinix, B. (2002). *Selecting and retaining teacher mentors* (Report No. Ed-SP-2002-05). Washington DC: ERIC Clearinghouse on Teaching and Teacher Education. (ERIC Document Reproduction Service No. ED477728).

National Center for History in Schools. (1994). *National standards for history thinking.* Retrieved June 21, 2006, from the World Wide Web: http://nchs.ucla.edu/standards/thinking5-12.html

O'Conner, J.E. & Jackson, M.A. (1988). *American history/American film.* New York, NY: Ungar Publishing Company.

Paris, M. (1997). *ERIC clearinghouse for social studies/social sci-
ence Education.* Bloomington, Indiana. (ERIC Document
Reproduction Service No. EDOSO9714).

Reform K-12. (2004). *Aren't classroom VCRs wonderful? Reform
K-12.* Retrieved September 7, 2006, from the World Wide
Web: http://www.reformk12.com/archives/000034.nclk

Robert, A. & Parchet, G. (1962). Do worksheets improve film
utilization? *AV Communication Review, 10,* 106-109.

Rosenstone, R.A. (1995). *Visions of the past: The challenge of film
to our idea of history.* Cambridge, MA: Harvard University
Press.

Santos, J.R. (1999, April). Cronbach's alpha: A tool for assessing
the reliability of scales. *Journal of Extension, 37(2).* Retrieved June 27, 2006, from the World Wide Web:
http://www.joe.org/joe/1999april/tt3.html

Smith, K. (1999). *Mental hygiene: Classroom films 1945-1970.*
New York, NY: Blast Books.

Smith, P., Roberts, K., & Taylor, C. (1973). *The use of inferred
objectives with the instructional films.* Tempe, AZ: Arizona
State University, College of Education. (ERIC Document
Reproduction Service No. ED072643).

Salomon, G. (1979). *The Interaction of Media, Cognition, and
Learning.* San Francisco, CA: Jossey-Bass Publishing.

Sumstine, D. (1918). "A comparative study of visual instruction in
the high school." *School and Society, 7,* 235-238.

United States Copyright Office. (1976). *Title 17 (1) Section 107 of
the Copyright Law of the United States; Limitations on exclusive rights: Fair use.* Retrieved October 5, 2006, from
the   World   Wide   Web: Fair   Use.
http://www.copyright.gov/title17/92chap1.html#107

———. (1976). *Title 17 (1) Section 110 of the Copyright Law of
the United States; Limitations on exclusive rights: Exemption of certain performances and displays.* Retrieved October 5, 2006, from the World Wide Web:
       http://www.copyright.gov/title17/92chap1.html#110

United States Government. (1981). Federal guidelines for off-air
recording of broadcast programming for educational purposes. *Congressional Record,* pp. E4750-E4752.

Wilson, W. & Herman, G. (1994). *American history on the screen: A teacher's resource book on film and video.* Portland, Maine: J. Weston Walch, Publisher.

Wise, H. (1939). *Motion pictures as an aid in teaching American history.* New Haven, CT: Yale University Press.

Wittich, W. (1953). Needed research in audio-visual methods. *AV Communication Review, 1,* 99-105.

INDEX

www.ingramcontent.com/pod-product-compliance
Lightning Source LLC
Chambersburg PA
CBHW021823270326
41932CB00007B/318